Crafts for all Abilities

For Nigel

*Thank you for all your positive support
and for seeing my initial ideas for
a book through to completion.*

*With thanks to all the people who have worked on the projects and
have allowed me to reproduce their work in this book.
Their ages range from 3¹/₂ to 102.*

Mr Fred Bailey, Phyl Bartlett, Mrs Josie Beady, Jenny Bentinck, Mary Betty,
Mrs Blake, Florence Bowditch, Simon Brignell, Mark Brinkworth,
Simone Brinkworth, Peggy Burdis, Marjorie Burman, Mrs Camp, Val Case,
Hester Causby, Mrs Churchward, Mrs C Cocksey, Ben Coffey, Emily Cooke,
Natasha Cooke, Anna Coombs, Jan Coombs, Rod Coombs, Sarah Coombs,
Kate Cooper, Philip Crossman, Richard Crossman, Ashley Day, Pauline Day,
Miss Mabel Dill, Dorothy Dowell, Miss Evelyn Down, Agnes Eglington,
Dot Ellery, Flo Foley, Peggy Ford, Kay Fuller, Lillian Goddard,
Rosemary Graham, Dilys Greatbatch, Esther Gutsell, Jean Hamley,
Ben Harland, Rhian Harman, Mrs Laura Harris, Mrs Grace Hill, Oliver Hill,
Ellen Howkins, Kathleen Hughes, Gill Jefferis, Ivy Jeffrey, Elsie King,
Grace Larson, Annie Lee, Pam McGinley, Margo McKnight, Emily Malins,
Rupert Malins, Mrs Beryl Mason, Tom Meade, Rebecca Miners, Mr A Mitchell,
Mrs Doreen Perry, Mrs Louie Pester, Bill Phillips, Elvis Pole,
Les Pole, Judy Pole, Steve Pole, Jane Powell, Joyce Pugh, Mrs Russell,
Betty Ryland, Jamie Sambells, Philip Sambells, Chloe Snuggs,
Mrs Elsie Stevens, Dimity Taiani, Joan Tatler, Emily Trent, Mrs Trixie Trewin, Sarah
Turner, Lily Twining, Ainsley Walcroft, Ryan Walcroft, Emily Walpole,
Mr Alex Ward, Mrs Connie Ward.

With thanks also to Abbotsbury Crafts Group; The Acorn Day Centre, Weymouth;
Chesil Beach Playgroup; Cheverells Residential Home, Northam;
Eastleigh Residential Home, South Molton; Glebelands Residential Home, Northam;
Portesham Crafts Group; and Portesham Primary School.

Crafts
for all Abilities

Sue Melville

SEARCH PRESS

First published in Great Britain 1997

Search Press Limited
Wellwood, North Farm Road,
Tunbridge Wells, Kent TN2 3DR

Reprinted 1998

ISBN 0 85532 822 3

Suppliers
If you have any difficulty in obtaining any of the
materials and equipment mentioned in this book, then
please write for a current list of stockists, including firms
who operate a mail-order service, to the Publishers:

Search Press Limited, Wellwood,
North Farm Road, Tunbridge Wells,
Kent TN2 3DR, England

Printed in Spain by Elkar S. Coop. Bilbao 48012

Contents

Introduction

The idea for this book came from my experience of working with different groups of people, but I soon realised that these projects could be adapted for individuals. Although I hope the book will appeal to all ages and abilities, it is especially suitable for anyone with limitations – the elderly, the very young or people with disabilities.

The projects are imaginative and designed to encourage a feel for colour and design, but it is possible to achieve impressive results even if you are not particularly artistic! I have tried to describe each project in a way that takes nothing for granted.

All the materials and tools needed for the projects are listed and there is also advice on how to adapt certain projects to create alternative pieces. Before you begin, it is worth bearing in mind that many of the projects can be quite messy, so make sure your work surfaces are well covered – plastic sheeting over newspaper is ideal.

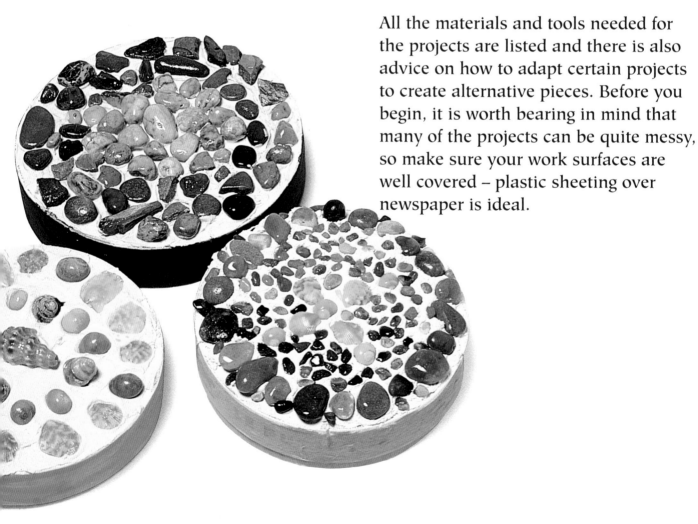

You will find a large range of projects and they draw on lots of different materials, all of which are easily obtainable – from making papier-mâché bowls using balloons as moulds, to creating trinket boxes out of shells; greetings cards from raffia and flowers; and plaques from salt dough. The clear step-by-step photographs will guide you through all the stages necessary to produce a whole range of attractive and useful objects – many of which make ideal gifts.

All these projects are designed for individuals, but they work equally well for groups. For this reason, you will find a special section on pages 8–9 aimed at carers, special needs teachers or anyone who wishes to teach a group or class.

Here, you will find lots of helpful tips and advice on how best to prepare for teaching your group.

Whether used as a form of therapy, to help recover forgotten skills, to boost shaky confidence or simply because you enjoy crafts, I hope you have fun with this book and find that it provides you with plenty of inspirational ideas.

All the items on these pages are included in the book. The shell boxes are featured on pages 56–57; the balloon bowls on pages 16–17; the découpage notebooks on pages 18–19; and the greetings cards on pages 36–41.

Working with groups

You can tackle all these projects on your own, but this book can also be used by anyone working with a group of people. If you are using the book with a group or class, you should take the following into account:

◆ When you have to provide equipment and materials for a group, it can get expensive. Look for cheaper alternatives – recycled material, cast-offs or off-cuts.

◆ Most of these projects can get quite messy, so make sure your work surfaces are well covered before you begin. I use plastic sheeting (mattress protectors) over newspaper.

◆ Try out every project yourself before doing it with a group. If your group has a limitation, imagine how you might cope with that limitation and adapt the project further if necessary.

◆ If you are working with elderly people, bear in mind that they often find it difficult to work on white background material, so use muted colours as far as possible.

◆ If you are working with elderly or disabled people, remember to allow for space between tables for wheelchairs, walking sticks or frames.

◆ Allow plenty of time for people to settle down before you start giving instructions.

◆ When you explain a project, make sure that anyone whose hearing or eyesight is limited is clear about what to do, and give them special encouragement if necessary.

◆ Let people talk as they work, to share experiences and to enjoy the pride of displaying finished masterpieces.

◆ Mark everybody's work with their name or initials at each stage, so you always know who has made what.

◆ If you are working with elderly or disabled people, make sure you have clean damp cloths and towels available at the end of the session – hands will need to be washed and dried so that wheelchairs, walking sticks and frames do not get messy.

◆ You may find you do not have time to clean all tools during the session – it is worth bringing plastic bags so you can take away any messy equipment.

◆ Enjoyment and stretching the imagination are more important than following a strict programme. I have found it better to finish off work myself discreetly than to let a project drag on.

These are some of the groups who made the crafts illustrated in this book: a playgroup, a primary school, two craft groups and a residential home for the elderly.

Before you start

Making a template

There are some projects in this book that involve the use of templates (see pages 18, 36, 40, 44, 49, 50 and 60). If you want to make a template bigger or smaller, adjust the size of the image in the book on a photocopier before following the steps below. For some projects, ready-made quilting templates are a good alternative.

Place a piece of tracing paper over the template image and hold it in place using masking tape. Draw around the image with a soft pencil. If you want to trace on to dark-coloured card, use a white pencil.

Turn the tracing paper over and firmly rub over the back of the line with your pencil.

Turn the tracing paper back over. Attach it to a piece of card using masking tape. Go around the outline again, pressing firmly with your pencil to transfer the image. Cut out the shape to produce a template.

Making a viewfinder

Cut out a rectangle of card, then cut out a smaller rectangle from the middle of the first one. Use this as a viewfinder to help you select the best part of a pattern. To make a round viewfinder, draw around large and small inverted cups or glasses.

Making a greetings card

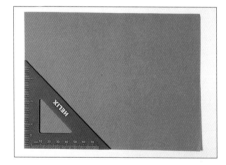

To make a basic greetings card, measure a rectangle 20 x 15cm (8 x 6in) on to thin card. Use a set square to ensure that all four corners are right angles. Cut the rectangle out and then fold it in half.

Cards in this book have been designed to measure 10 x 15cm (4 x 6in) when folded; this size will fit into a standard envelope.

If you want to make a bigger card, remember to check that it will fit inside your envelope before cutting out.

WORKING WITH PAPER

Collage plates

Papier-mâché napkin rings

Balloon bowls

Découpage notebooks

Collage boxes

Collage plates

Torn shreds of paper are glued to paper plates

You will need

Cardboard picnic plate
Glossy magazine
PVA glue
Scissors
Glue brush

Preparation

Before you start, tear a few sheets from a glossy magazine into small pieces. Sort out the pieces into piles of different colours and decide which colour or colours you would like to concentrate on.

As this project involves a lot of glue, it is a good idea to cover your work surface before you begin.

This colourful collage project transforms paper plates.

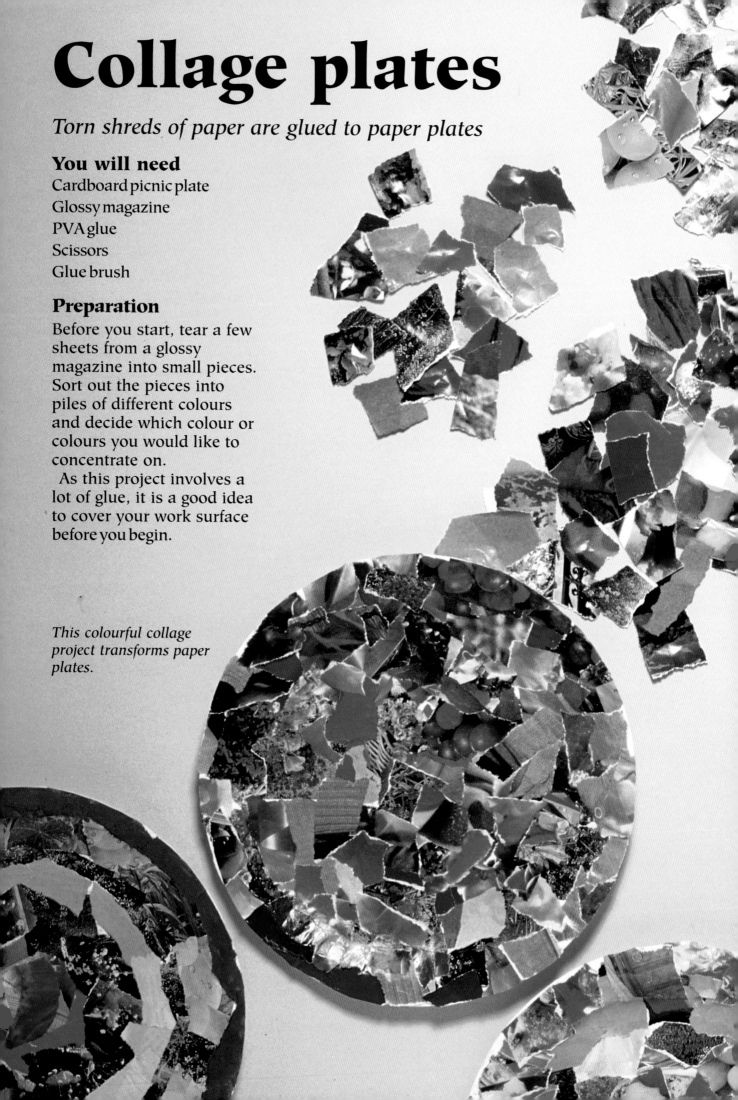

1 Glue pieces of paper in your chosen colour scheme on to a cardboard picnic plate. Gradually build up a collage by overlapping piece upon piece until the whole plate is covered.

2 Carefully trim around the edge of the plate with scissors. Ensure that each piece of paper is firmly glued down before brushing the top of the plate with a generous coat of glue.

Papier-mâché napkin rings

Papier-mâché is applied to cardboard tubes and finished with oil pastels

You will need

Cardboard tube
Scissors
Ruler
Pencil
Masking tape
Wallpaper paste
Newspaper
Paint brush

White paint
Oil pastels
PVA glue
Glue brush

1 To make one napkin ring, cut two rings 3cm (1¼in) wide from a cardboard tube. Open up one of the rings and fit the other inside it.

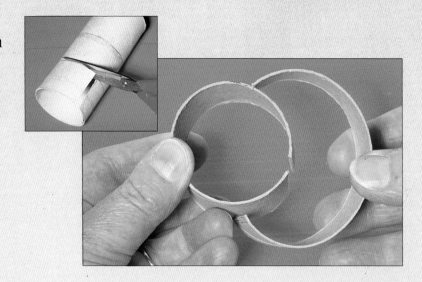

2 Gently ease the rings out to a diameter of approximately 5cm (2in) then bind them together with masking tape to form a single ring.

3 Make up a small amount of wallpaper paste following the instructions on the packet. Brush the paste on to thin strips of newspaper. Wrap one strip at a time around the ring. Continue, until you have built up three layers. Leave to dry for twenty-four hours.

4 Apply a coat of white paint to the inside of the ring. Leave to dry before painting the outside. When this is dry, repeat.

5 Colour the outside of the ring using oil pastels. When you are happy with the design, gently rub over it with your fingers to blend the colours. Varnish by applying a coat of PVA glue.

You can decorate your napkin ring with pictures from a magazine, or personalize it with your initial. You could also paint the inside of the ring to complement the outside.

Balloon bowls

Balloons are used as moulds to create unusual papier-mâché bowls

To make bigger and stronger bowls, build up more layers of papier-mâché and paint gesso over the dried papier-mâché before painting. Make sure your base is strong enough to support the bowl – a wooden cheese box lid works well for large bowls.

You will need

Round balloon
Drawing pin
Block of wood
Large jar
Newspaper
Wallpaper paste
Paint brush
Large cardboard tube
Masking tape
White paint
Coloured paint
PVA glue
Glue brush

1 Blow up a balloon to the size of a small watermelon and knot the end. Fix the knot to a block of wood using a drawing pin and then place it inside a jar. Pinning the balloon to the wood will stop it moving around while you work, and you can hold the jar between your knees when you are applying the papier-mâché.

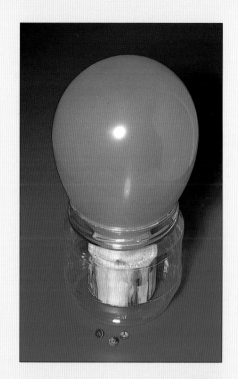

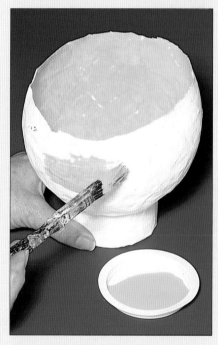

2 Make up a small amount of wallpaper paste following the instructions on the packet. Tear several sheets of newspaper into small pieces. Brush wallpaper paste on to each piece and stick them one by one to the top of the balloon. Continue until you are half way down the balloon. Leave to dry.

3 Cut out a base from a cardboard tube and position it on top of the balloon. When you are sure that it is level, secure it in place with masking tape. Apply papier-mâché over the base then build up several more layers over the whole bowl. Leave to dry for at least twenty-four hours, then remove the balloon.

4 Paint the inside of the bowl with white paint. When dry, paint the outside. Repeat, using a coloured paint of your choice. Decorate your bowl using coloured paints, stencils, gold felt-tips or torn coloured paper. Varnish with a layer of PVA glue.

Découpage notebooks

Notebooks are decorated with colourful cut-outs

You will need

Tracing paper
White card
Pencil
Scissors
White paper, A4 (12 x 8in)
Gold or silver pen
Felt-tip pens
Notebook
Glue stick
PVA glue
Glue brush
Glitter glue stick
Small beads

Preparation

Trace the elephant and flower shown above on to thin white card (see page 10). Cut out the shapes to produce templates.

  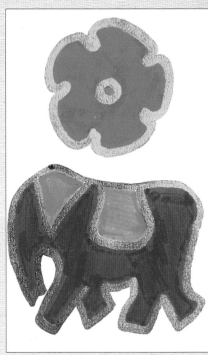

1 Place the templates on to white paper and draw around them with a pencil. Repeat until you have enough images to cover your notebook.

2 Cover the pencil lines with gold or silver pen.

3 Colour the images in with felt-tip pens, then carefully cut them all out.

4 Arrange the cut-out images to overlap and cover the front and back of the notebook. When you are happy with the design, stick the images down using a glue stick. Decorate with beads and a glitter glue stick. When dry, varnish with PVA glue.

This technique can be used to decorate folders, writing paper, pen holders or gift boxes.

Collage boxes

Unusual boxes are made from card, decorated with collage and lined with tissue paper

You can use these boxes for gifts, jewellery or pot-pourri. As an alternative to collaging with paper from magazines, try using tissue paper, pushed into wrinkles. You could decorate boxes with photocopies of family photographs or lots of photocopies of your signature. To achieve an antique look, soak the photocopies in tea, then allow them to dry before gluing in place.

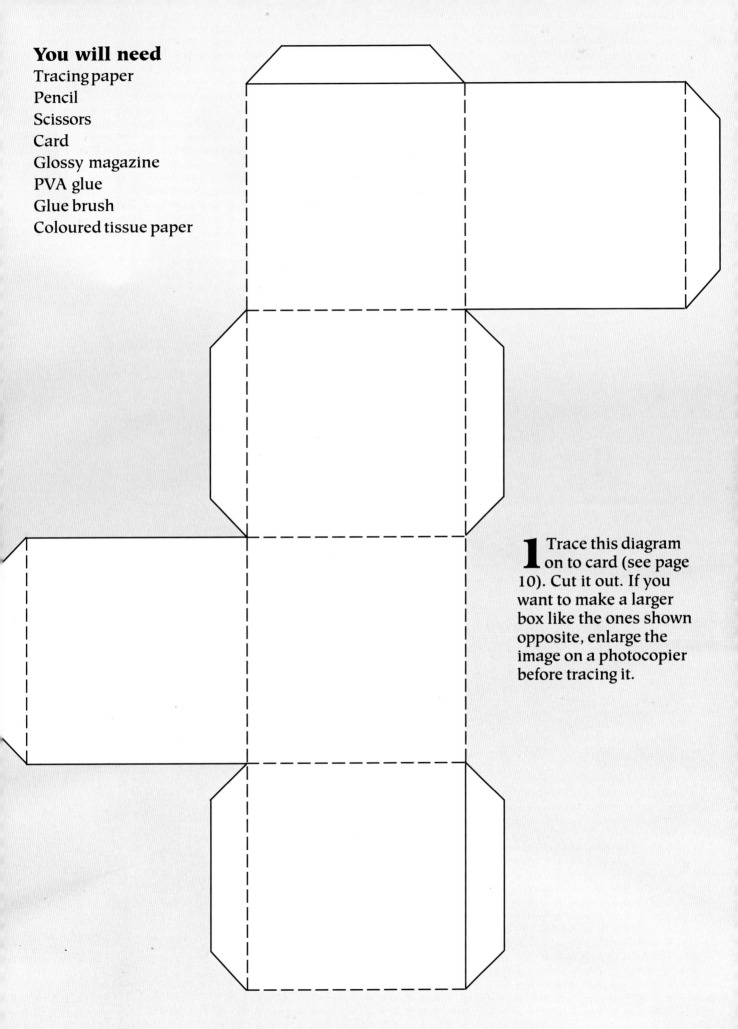

You will need

Tracing paper
Pencil
Scissors
Card
Glossy magazine
PVA glue
Glue brush
Coloured tissue paper

1 Trace this diagram on to card (see page 10). Cut it out. If you want to make a larger box like the ones shown opposite, enlarge the image on a photocopier before tracing it.

2 Tear a few sheets from a glossy magazine into small pieces, then sort out the pieces into piles of different colours. Glue pieces from your chosen colour scheme on to the cut-out shape. Trim the edges.

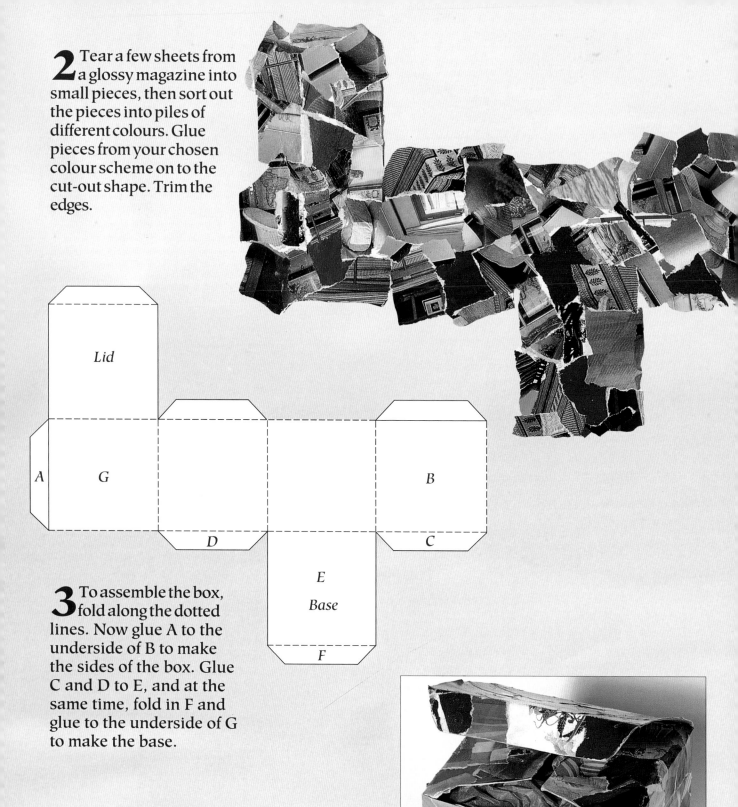

Lid

A | G | B

D | C

E
Base

F

3 To assemble the box, fold along the dotted lines. Now glue A to the underside of B to make the sides of the box. Glue C and D to E, and at the same time, fold in F and glue to the underside of G to make the base.

4 Varnish the outside of the assembled box with PVA glue. When this is dry, line the inside loosely with coloured tissue paper.

WORKING WITH FABRIC

Embroidered coasters

Lavender bags

Woven bags

Woollen squares and pom-poms

Embroidered coasters

These designs are worked in wool using a variety of stitches

You will need

Soft pencil

Ruler

Binka canvas

Scissors

Felt-tip pens

Tapestry needle

Selection of double knitting wools

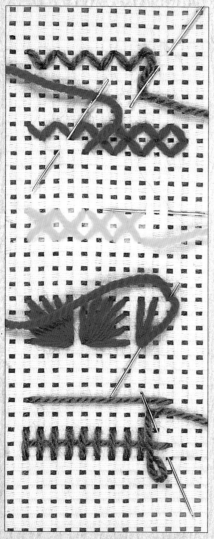

A selection of straight stitches that can be used for this project.

Preparation

Coarse mesh binka canvas is ideal for this project. It is easy to work with this material; stitches can be unpicked and reworked quickly and without any difficulty, and the edges fray easily.

It is easier to embroider a design if the colours of the felt-tip pens and the wools match. Choose colours that complement each other and embroider over the designs, using the felt-tip colours as a guide.

If you have never tried canvas work before, start by practising the stitches shown here on a spare piece of canvas. When you feel confident enough to start embroidering, follow the stages opposite.

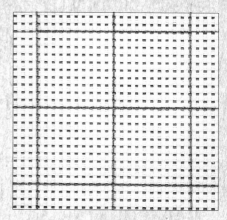

1 Draw a square approximately 12 x 12cm (4³⁄₄ x 4³⁄₄in) on to binka canvas using a soft pencil and a ruler. Make sure the pencil lines follow the weave of the fabric. Cut the square out carefully. Draw a border four rows in from the main square all round to allow for the frayed edge. Divide the inner square into quarters to find the centre.

2 Work from the stitch sampler opposite and use felt-tip pens to sketch out your design ideas on to a piece of paper. When you are satisfied with the design, copy it on to the canvas.

3 Stitch your design on to the canvas using the stitches shown opposite. Match the wool colours with the felt-tip pen colours and work from the centre of the design to the outside.

4 Gently pull the canvas threads away from the edges of the stitched design to create a frayed border.

These stitched designs can be used as coasters, table mats or plant pot stands. There are lots of different stitches you can use in conjunction with the ones shown in this project.

Lavender bags

Transfer crayons are used on fine fabric

You will need

18cm (7in) plate	Fine white synthetic fabric	Tablespoon
Pencil	Transfer crayons	Dried lavender
Scissors	White paper	Elastic bands
Tracing paper	Iron	Narrow ribbon
Masking tape		

1 Place a plate on top of a sheet of tracing paper and draw round the rim.

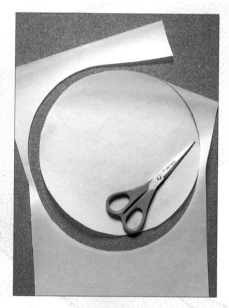

2 Cut out the circle of tracing paper.

3 Tape a piece of white fabric to your work surface. Repeat stages 1 and 2 to get a circle of fabric.

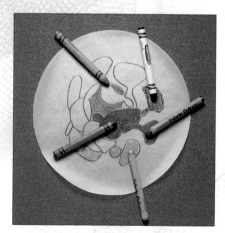

4 Draw a pattern on to the tracing paper (you could use a design as on pages 36–37). Colour it in with transfer crayons.

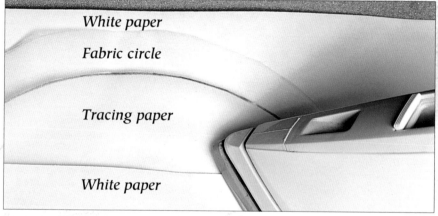

White paper

Fabric circle

Tracing paper

White paper

5 Place a piece of white paper on your ironing board to protect it. Put the coloured side of the tracing paper against the right side of the fabric circle and then put both on top of the white paper. Put another sheet of white paper on top.

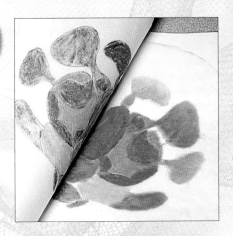

6 Iron over the tracing paper to transfer the design on to the fabric.

7 With the fabric circle wrong side up, place a tablespoon of lavender in the centre.

8 Pull the edges of the fabric circle together and secure them half way down with an elastic band.

You can experiment with lots of different colours and designs when making these lavender bags. For an original pattern, try taking a rubbing from textured paper.

9 Wrap a strip of narrow ribbon on top of the elastic band. Tie the ribbon in a bow and trim the ends, allowing for 7cm (2³⁄₄in) to hang down.

Woven bags

Felt and ribbon is woven to make small bags

You will need

Ribbon 1.25cm (½in) wide

Felt

Ruler

Scissors

Tailor's chalk

PVA glue

Clothes-pegs

Glue brush

Preparation

You will need 2m (6½ft) of ribbon in all. Out of this you will need to cut six 16cm (6¼in) lengths and six 9cm (3in) lengths to make the bag. You will need an 8cm (3in) and a 37cm (14½in) length to make the fastener.

These attractive bags require no sewing. Try adjusting the measurements to make a bigger bag. If you use longer lengths of ribbon at the sides, you can tie with bows. Some ribbon comes with a slightly stiffened edge, which will help the bows to keep their shape.

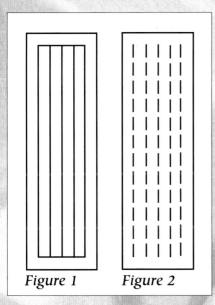
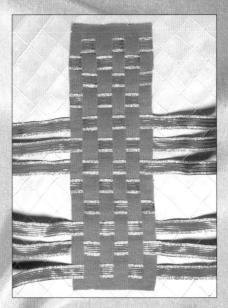

Figure 1   Figure 2

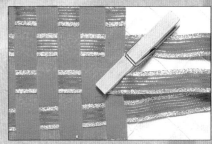

1 Cut out a rectangle of felt 29 x 9cm (11½ x 3in). Use a piece of tailor's chalk and a ruler to draw a border 1.5cm (½in) in from the edge all round. Draw three lines 1.5cm (½in) apart down the length of the felt up to the border (figure 1).

Carefully cut along the five lines (figure 2).

2 Beginning at one end, weave four of the short strands of ribbon in and out of the felt, then three of the long lengths of ribbon, leaving equal lengths of ribbon on both sides. Now weave in the two remaining short pieces and finally the last three long pieces.

3 Fix the ribbon to the felt at each end with a blob of glue. Attach clothes-pegs to hold the ribbon in place until the glue is dry.

4 Turn up the bottom of the felt so that the long ribbons are opposite each other. Glue the sides and then tie the ribbon with knots. Trim the ends.

5 Fold the 8cm (3in) length of ribbon in half and glue this underneath the ribbon at the front of the flap to make a loop. Hold in place with a clothes peg until dry. Thread the 37cm (14½in) length of ribbon through the woven felt or ribbon on the front of the bag and tie with a bow to secure the flap of the bag.

Woollen squares and pom-poms

Squares are woven on a handmade loom and simple pom-poms are made from wool

You will need

Card
Sharp scissors
Ruler
Pencil

Coloured wools
Sticky tape
Tapestry needle

Finished squares can be sewn together to make a colourful rug. Hand-stitch or machine the squares on to a backing fabric.

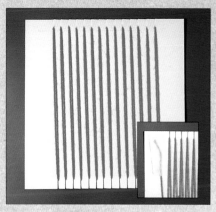

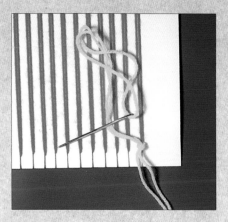

1 Cut out a square from card. Make sure it is 2.5cm (1 in) larger all round than you want your finished square to be. Cut slits in the card at two ends to make a loom. Secure an end of the wool on to the back of the loom with sticky tape and then wind the wool twice around each notch. Cut off the wool and secure the end with sticky tape.

2 Thread a tapestry needle with wool. Tie the end on to the first double strand of wool on the loom.

3 Weave the wool in and out of the loom. Change colours when you wish. Do not pull the wool too tight, or the square will distort.

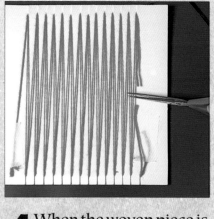

4 When the woven piece is finished, turn the loom over and cut the wool down the centre.

5 Darn all the loose ends in to the woven square, leaving about 2cm (³/₄in) of wool.

6 Pull the ends of the wool taut, then trim them off.

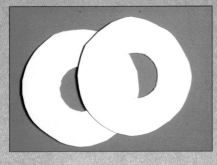

1 Cut out two circles of card with smaller circles inside. The size of the circles will decide the size of your pom-poms.

2 Put the circles of card together and then wind wool around them.

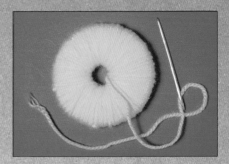

3 When the circle in the middle becomes very narrow, use a needle to thread the wool through.

4 Slip the scissors between the circles of card and cut the wool all around.

5 Tie a piece of wool tightly between the circles of card. If you leave the ends long, you can use them to attach the pom-pom to a rug. Snip through the card and remove it.

A rug can be edged with ribbon and then decorated with pom-poms in a matching colour. These pom-poms were made by a lady aged one hundred and two.

GREETINGS CARDS

Fallen leaves

Overlapping shapes

Potato-printed shapes

Collage cats

Dried flowers and raffia

Silver stars

Christmas trees

Stained glass windows

Shapes and dots

Fallen leaves

Colourful leaves are used to make attractive cards

You will need
Thin red card
Thin white card
Pencil
Ruler
Scissors
Fallen leaves
White paper
PVA glue
Glue brush

Preparation
Collect fallen leaves of different colours and sizes. These can be stored in an airtight container, but it is best to use them as soon as possible after collecting them. You should not dry or press the leaves.

1 Cut out a greetings card from the red card and fold it in half (see page 10). Measure then cut out a rectangle of white card 1cm (½in) smaller all round than the front of the folded red card.

2 Cut out a piece of white paper roughly the same size as the white card. Arrange a selection of leaves on the white paper. When you are happy with the design, dab each leaf with glue, and transfer them on to the white card.

3 Glue the white card on to the front of the red card, ensuring that the border is even all around. Carefully brush each leaf with PVA glue, taking care not to get glue on the card itself.

Calendar

Leaves are versatile and can also be used to make original calendars or bookmarks. This calendar has been made from mounting board, and plaited raffia has been used to make a hanging loop. Bookmarks can be covered with clear plastic film to protect the leaves.

35

Overlapping shapes

Brightly coloured random patterns are made from templates

You will need

Tracing paper
Thin white card
Pencil
Scissors
White paper
Coloured felt-tip pens
Small and large glass
Coloured paper
Thin coloured card
Glue stick

Preparation

Cut out a greetings card from the coloured card and fold it in half (see page 10).

Trace the square and round shapes shown here on to a piece of thin white card. Cut out the shapes to produce templates.

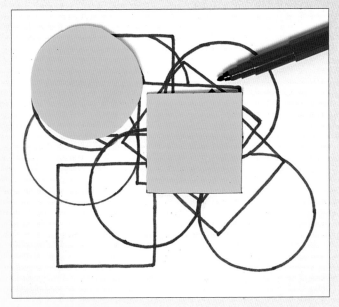

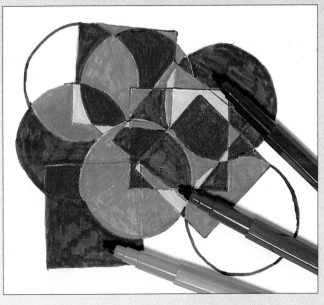

1 Place the square template on white paper and draw around it with a felt-tip pen. Continue, moving the template each time. Repeat using the round template.

2 Colour your design with felt-tip pens.

3 Use a small glass or a circular viewfinder (see page 10) to help you select the best area of your design. Draw around the glass with a felt-tip pen and cut out the shape.

4 Place a large glass on coloured paper. Draw around it, and cut out the shape. Glue your design on to the coloured paper circle, then glue this on to the front of your greetings card.

You could use circles, squares or triangles for your templates, or quilting templates for more elaborate designs. Try experimenting with random freehand patterns or varying the thickness of the felt-tip pens to produce bolder designs. You could also draw the designs on coloured paper but remember that this can affect the colours produced by the felt-tip pens.

Potato-printed shapes

Potatoes and bright coloured paints are used to create hand-printed cards

You will need
Thin blue card
Potato
Kitchen knife
Sponge
Coloured paint
Red sugar paper
Soft pencil
Ruler
Scissors
Glue stick
Sequins

Preparation
Cut out the greetings card from the blue card and fold it in half (see page 10).

1 Cut a potato in half. Use a knife to score a simple shape into the centre of one of the halves. Now cut away the outside surrounding area to a depth of 0.5cm (¼in).

2 Gently dab a sponge into the paint and then apply to your potato.

3 Use the potato to print on to the sugar paper and gradually build up a design. If you like, you can clean the sponge and then add to your design using a different colour.

4 When the paint is dry, select the best area of your design using a view-finder (see page 10). Cut out a shape of your choice.

5 Glue your shape to the front of the card. Stick sequins on to the design and around the border.

Potatoes are cheap and make excellent block-printers. Gouache, powder paint or ready-mixed poster paint are ideal for this project. You can also use this printing method to make your own gift wrap. Experiment with mounting the design on to coloured sugar paper before sticking it on to the front of the card.

Collage cats

*Cards are made using silhouettes
and colourful collages*

You will need

Thin white card
Thin black card
Thin coloured card
Tracing paper
Dark and light-coloured
 pencil

Small sharp scissors or
 craft knife
Eraser
Ruler
Glossy magazine
PVA glue and glue brush

Preparation

Make up two greetings cards
from the thin coloured card
(see page 10).

1 Trace the cat shown
above on to a piece of
thin white card (see page
10). Cut it out to make a
template then place it in
the centre of a piece of
black card 12 x 10cm (4³/₄ x
4in). Draw around the
template with a light-
coloured pencil then
carefully cut out the shape.
Rub out any pencil marks
and keep both the positive
and negative images.

Positive   *Negative*

2 Cut out a piece of thin
white card 20 x 13cm (8
x 5in). Build up a collage on
the card by sticking down
small pieces torn from a
glossy magazine (see pages
12–13).

3 Carefully position the two black shapes on to the collage and then stick them down using PVA glue. Cut the collage in half and trim the edges neatly. Position your designs on to the greetings cards and then glue them down.

These cards work well using pictures from glossy magazines, newspapers, railway timetables or any other printed material – small type looks most effective. You could also build up a collage using gold crepe paper or even hand-painted paper.

Dried flowers and raffia

Natural materials are used to make attractive designs

You will need

Selection of dried flowers or
  grasses with strong stems
Thin cream card
Ruler
Pencil
Double-sided tape
Large and small glass
Scissors
Raffia

Preparation

You can buy dried flowers
and grasses from florists,
and raffia is available from
garden centres and craft
shops. You could choose to
collect a selection of
hedgerow flowers and
grasses yourself – it is best
to pick them once they
have dried naturally,
towards the end of the year.
Make sure that they have
strong stems so that they
can be woven into the
raffia.

Before you start you will
need to cut out a greetings
card (see page 10) from the
cream card. Fold it in half.

1 Attach a 6cm (2¼in)
strip of double-sided
tape to the front of the
card.

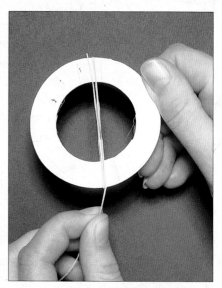

2 Use a small and large
inverted glass to mark
an inner and outer circle on
a piece of card. Cut the
shape out. Position eight
small pieces of double-sided
tape at equal distances
around the circle. Wind a
short length of raffia around
the circle and on to two
opposite pieces of tape.

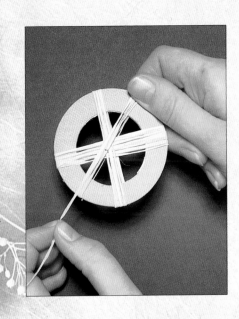

3 Wind four pieces of raffia in total. When complete, snip all the ends.

4 Weave flowers and dried grasses through the raffia. Attach the woven circle to the double-sided tape on the cream card.

As an alternative to wrapping raffia around a circle of card, try knitting a piece of raffia and weaving dried flowers and grasses into this.

43

Silver stars

Striking cards can be made with silver wrapping paper, sequins and glitter

You will need
Tracing paper
White card
Soft pencil
Scissors
Thin blue card
Silver wrapping paper or foil
Glue stick
Glitter
Sequins

Preparation
Cut out a greetings card from thin blue card and fold it in half (see page 10).

1 Trace the two stars shown here on to white card (see page 10). Cut out the shapes to produce templates.

2 Place the large star template on silver wrapping paper and the small one on blue card. Draw around the stars and then cut out the shapes.

3 Glue the silver star on to the front of the greetings card. Overlap the blue star then glue it in place. Decorate the card by dabbing on glue and applying glitter and sequins. When the glue is dry, shake the card to remove excess glitter.

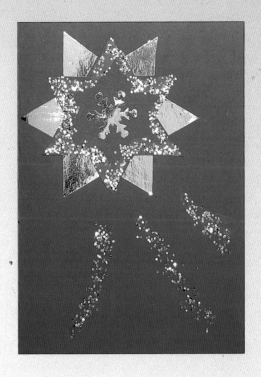

Many different designs can be created using silver wrapping paper, glitter and sequins. Silver foil can be used in place of silver wrapping paper if you wish. You can enrich cards further by using gold and silver pens.

Christmas trees

Doilies, sequins and tissue paper are used to make cards and matching gift wrap

You will need

Thin green card
Thin red card
Circular paper doily
White tissue paper
Sponge
Green poster paint
Scissors
Pencil
Ruler
Glue stick
Glitter
Sequins

Preparation

Cut out the greetings card from green card (see page 10). Cut out a piece of red card 12 x 8cm (4³/₄ x 3¹/₄in) and glue this to the front of the green card.

One doily will make approximately eight greetings cards and this attractive matching gift wrap can be made at the same time.

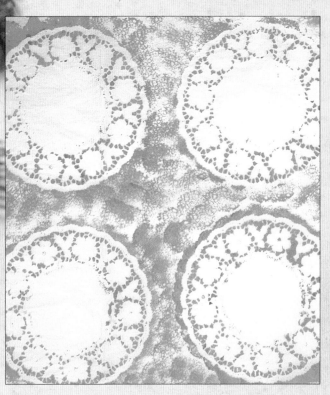

1 Lay the doily on top of white tissue paper and sponge on green paint.

2 To make matching gift wrap, continue dabbing, moving the doily until you have covered the tissue paper in an attractive design. Put the tissue paper on one side to dry.

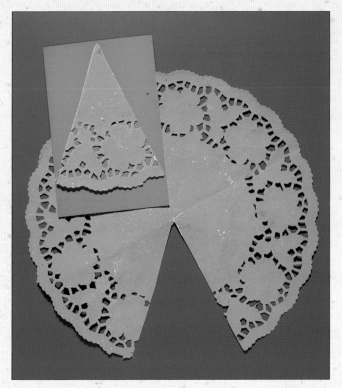

3 Fold the doily into quarters to find the centre. Cut out a slice to fit on to your red rectangle. Glue in place.

4 Cut out a small square from the green card to make the base of the tree; glue it in place. Dab glue on to the tree and apply glitter and sequins.

Stained glass windows

A cellophane collage is built up to make stained glass windows

You will need

Thin coloured card	Clear cellophane
Tracing paper	Coloured cellophane
Soft pencil	Glue stick
Ruler	Double-sided tape
Scissors	

1 Cut out a greetings card from coloured card and fold it in half (see page 10). Trace the design shown here on to the front of the card (see page 10). Cut out the design carefully using a pair of small sharp scissors or a craft knife.

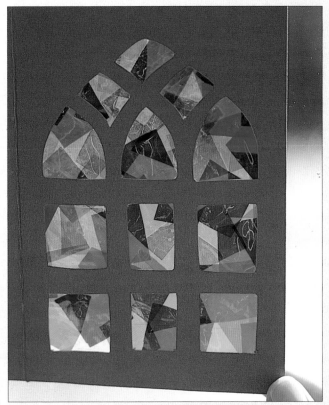

2 Cut out a piece of clear cellophane 18 x 23cm (7 x 9in). Cut out small pieces of coloured cellophane then glue them on to the clear cellophane to build up a collage.

3 Decide on the best position for your cellophane collage by placing it under the cut-out design and holding it up to the light. Stick in place using double-sided tape. Trim off any excess cellophane.

Shapes and dots

Templates are used on patterns made from felt-tip dots

You will need
Thin coloured card
Thin white card
Tracing paper
Felt-tip pens
White paper
Ruler
Pencil
Scissors
Glue stick

Preparation
Before you begin, trace the shapes shown here on to thin white card (see page 10). Cut out the shapes to produce templates.
 Cut out a greetings card from the coloured card and fold it in half (see page 10).

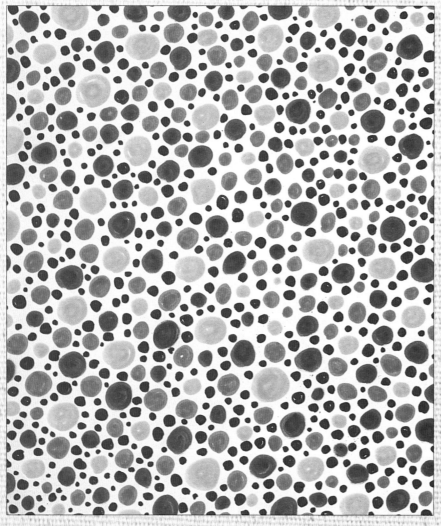

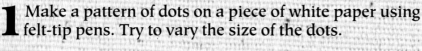

1 Make a pattern of dots on a piece of white paper using felt-tip pens. Try to vary the size of the dots.

2 Arrange the templates on top of your design. Carefully draw round them using a felt-tip pen. Cut out the shapes.

3 Arrange the shapes on to the front of the greetings card. When you are happy with the design, glue in place.

These unusual designs make striking greetings cards, but they can also be used to brighten up notebook covers, or they can be framed as pictures. Try using wax crayons instead of felt-tip pens and washing over your pattern of dots with a coloured ink for a more dramatic effect.

OTHER PROJECTS

String savers

Decorated containers are used for storing balls of string

You will need

Container with plastic lid
Sandpaper
Paint brush
White poster paint
Coloured poster paint
Double-sided tape
String
Sharp instrument
Small sharp scissors
PVA glue

1 Lightly rub down the outside of the container with sandpaper to prepare it for painting.

2 Apply a coat of white poster paint and leave to dry.

3 Apply a coat of poster paint in the colour of your choice. Allow to dry.

4 Wind double-sided tape around the bottom 2.5cm (1in) section of the container. Cut a square of tape and stick it just above the taped section.

5 Starting at the bottom, wind string over the tape. Twirl a small length of string over the square of tape to finish off. Varnish the container with a coat of PVA glue. Leave to dry.

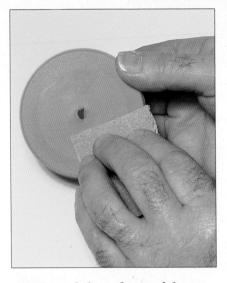
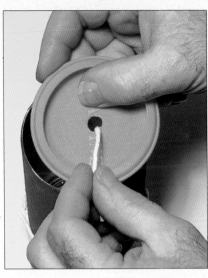

6 Pierce a small hole in the centre of the container's lid with a sharp instrument. Enlarge the hole by snipping it carefully with sharp scissors.

7 Sand the edges of the hole so that there are no rough pieces of plastic.

8 Place a ball of string inside the container and thread the end through the hole in the lid.

These colourful containers are an excellent way of storing balls of string. You can decorate your tins using coloured paint.

Shell boxes

Shells and pebbles are used to create trinket or jewellery boxes

You will need
Round box with lid
Shells and pebbles
Ready-mixed plaster filler
Spatula
Paint brush
Poster paint or emulsion paint
PVA glue

Preparation
Collect a variety of pebbles and shells. Before you start, wash and dry them and then sort them into piles of different colours, shapes and sizes. Start thinking about how you would like to arrange them into a design. Try to avoid using large pebbles as these will make your finished box too heavy.

1 Place a generous blob of plaster filler on to the lid of the box. Use a spatula to smooth out the plaster filler and cover the lid of the box evenly.

Wooden or cardboard cheese boxes are ideal for this project and are quickly transformed into attractive containers.

2 Arrange your design quickly on to the lid. Leave the filler to dry.

3 Paint the sides and underside of the box and the rim of the lid in a colour of your choice. Line the box with tissue paper that complements the outside colour. Apply two coats of PVA glue to the top of the lid.

Clay pots

Pots are made using coil and pinch methods

You will need
Air-drying clay
Water
Paint brush
Knife
Coloured poster paints
Water-based varnish

Preparation
You can buy air-drying clay from most craft shops. It does not need to be fired, but instead hardens naturally when left in contact with air.

For both pots, you will need a ball of clay about the size of a small orange.

When painted in colourful designs, these small pots make ideal presents – they will not, however, hold water. Experiment with making different pots. To make a slab pot, cut out a square for the base and four rectangles for the sides. Stick the pot together with water and use tiny sausages of clay to strengthen the joins inside.

Pinch pot

1 Roll your clay into a ball, then press your thumb into the centre to make a hollow.

2 Pinch the sides to make the hollow bigger. Stand the pot on your work surface and flatten the base with your thumb. Leave to dry.

The finished pinch pot
You can now choose to leave the pot plain or you could paint it with poster paints and then varnish it.

Coil pot

 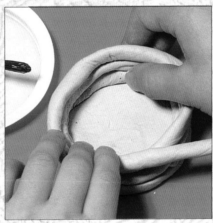 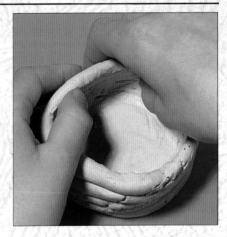

1 Flatten a ball of clay with your hands to make a circular base about 0.5cm (¼in) thick.

2 Make sausages with the rest of the clay. Coil them around the edge of the base. Brush water on to each layer before coiling the next one.

3 Use a little water and your finger to smooth the coils inside. Repeat on the outside for a smooth effect or use a knife to make a pattern. Leave to dry.

The finished coil pot, *ready for painting and varnishing.*

Salt dough plaques

Simple ingredients are used to make colourful plaques

You will need

3 cups plain flour	Wooden spoon	Scissors	Coloured paint
1 cup water	Rolling pin	Kitchen knife	Paint brush
1 cup cooking salt	Tracing paper	Garlic press	Hanger
Drizzle of oil	Thin card	Aluminium foil	All-purpose glue
Bowl	Pencil	Baking tray	Water-based varnish

1 Put the flour, water and salt into a bowl, pour on a drizzle of oil and mix well. Form into a ball and then roll out to a thickness of approximately 0.5cm (¼in)

2 Trace the house shown here on to thin card (see page 10). Cut out the shape to make a template.

3 Place the template on top of the dough and cut around it with a knife.

4 From the remaining dough, make a small rectangle for the door, thin sausages for the windows, and a small ball of dough for the door knob. Stick in place by brushing with water.

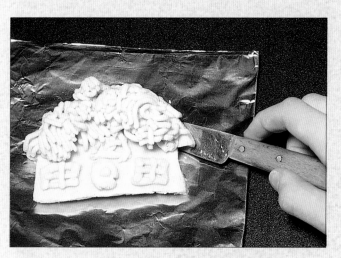

5 Break the remaining dough into small balls. Feed each of these balls through the garlic press, and use the strands for the thatched roof.

6 Put the plaque on foil and place on a baking tray. Bake for three hours at 100ºC (210ºF). Remove from the oven and leave to cool.

7 Paint the plaque using colours of your choice. When dry, varnish the front and back. Attach a small hanger to the back of the plaque with all-purpose glue.

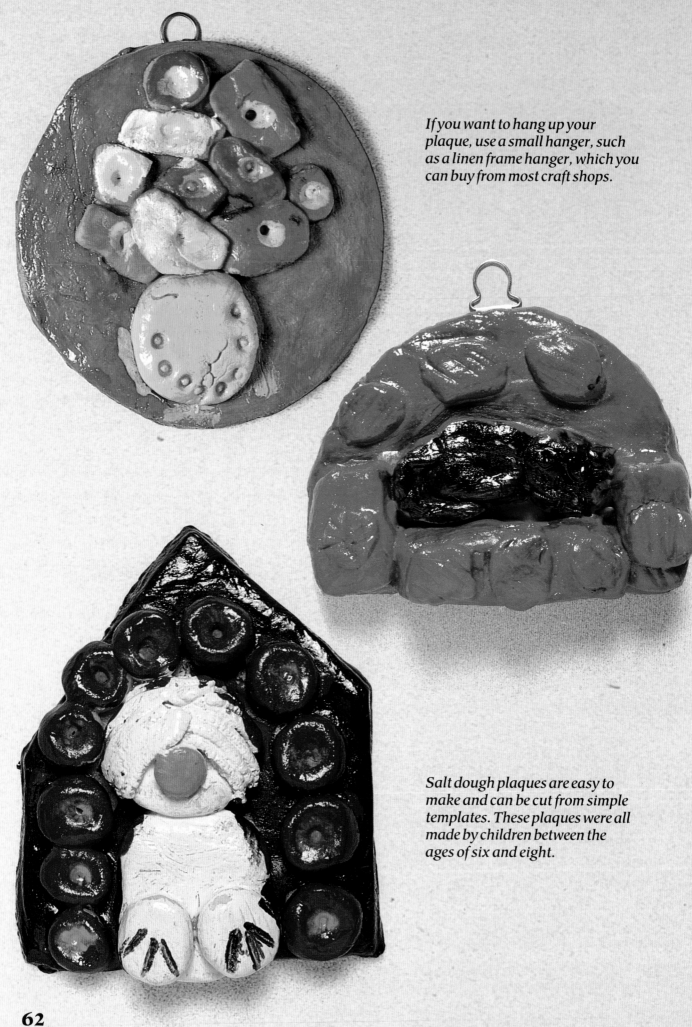

If you want to hang up your plaque, use a small hanger, such as a linen frame hanger, which you can buy from most craft shops.

Salt dough plaques are easy to make and can be cut from simple templates. These plaques were all made by children between the ages of six and eight.

Dried-flower pots

Flowers and grasses are used to make attractive table decorations

You will need
Margarine tub
Oasis
Bread knife
Small pebbles
Dried flowers and grasses

Preparation
Oasis is used as the base for these decorations. You can buy this from florists, together with dried flowers and grasses.

To dry flowers and grasses that you have collected yourself, tie them in a bunch and hang them upside down for about two weeks.

1 Use a bread knife to cut the oasis so that it fits snugly inside a margarine tub.

2 Push the stems of the flowers and grasses into the oasis. When you are happy with the arrangement, fill the gaps between the stems with small pebbles.

These flower arrangements make attractive table decorations or they can be used to brighten up a window sill, especially if the containers are decorated.

63

Index